MICRO WORLD

Microscopic Life
in the
Home

BRIAN WARD

W
FRANKLIN WATTS
LONDON • SYDNEY

Contents and definitions

Bacteria

Bacteria are tiny organisms, far too small to be seen without a microscope. They live just about everywhere. Bacteria may be rounded, thread-like or rod-shaped, and some of them can creep about, using waving threads called flagella. Some bacteria need oxygen to live, while others are killed by oxygen in the air.

Mites

We share our homes with millions of tiny spider-like creatures called mites, living in bedding and carpets. They do not cause any damage, but they can be a health risk.

Protista

Protista are microscopic organisms. We use the remains of some of these organisms, called diatoms, to make useful cleaning substances for the home.

Viruses

Viruses are even tinier than bacteria. Unlike many bacteria, viruses always have to infect a living cell if they are to grow and reproduce. They take over the whole of the workings of the cell and turn it into a virus factory, usually killing the cell as the new viruses are released.

Fungi

Fungi are small organisms that mostly feed on dead and decaying material. Tiny fungi called yeasts and moulds are used to prepare many useful food substances. But moulds also cause mildew that damages stored foods or makes ugly stains on damp walls in the home.

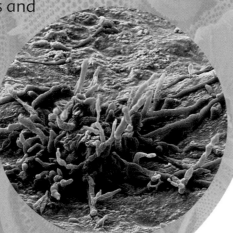

Sharing our homes with microbes

We spend a lot of time in our homes. But did you know that we share our homes with a huge number of microbes and the biological materials that they produce?

House-mates

These are some of the microbes that live with us at home:

- bacteria and viruses floating in the air and covering every surface in the home
- tiny dust mites living in carpets and beds
- fungi and their spores
- pollen drifting in the air
- small insects and their larvae.

You cannot get rid of these bugs, most of which are harmless anyway, but you can keep their numbers down by normal household cleaning. In particular, it is important to take steps to keep down the numbers of bugs that contaminate food and cause food poisoning.

◄ *Surfaces where food is prepared must be cleaned to remove microbes that grow on them.*

Babies and bacteria

Babies are most at risk of picking up infections in the home, so things such as feeding bottles and changing mats must be kept especially clean. Once babies start to crawl, it is impossible to keep them away from bacteria that are present in carpets or on the floor. Babies easily pick up infections, but usually they recover quickly and become immune to the effects of bacteria in the home.

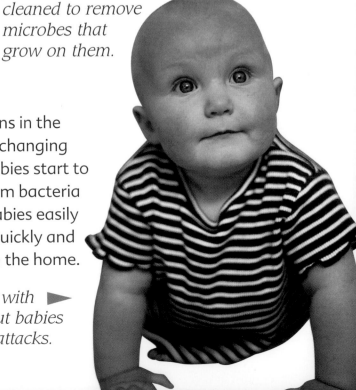

The floor in your home is thick with ► bacteria and other microbes, but babies soon become immune to their attacks.

Immunity

Since we are constantly exposed to bugs, the body's ability to become immune to their effects is an important natural process. Some people think that our homes are now too clean and bug-free, so our immune system never has to work very hard, and that this might have something to do with the increase in allergies and asthma.

Many cases of asthma are thought to be caused by exposure to house dust mites and their wastes. Once a person has asthma, even outdoor activities can bring on an attack. ▶

TRY IT YOURSELF

Spot the dangers

Look at this picture. How many dangers from micro-organisms can you spot? How can this kitchen be made safer for the baby?

Hazardous homes

It is only recently that people have been concerned about hygiene in the home, even though the idea that bugs could spread infection first developed more than 100 years ago. Yet our 'clean', modern homes probably contain just as many microbes and other bugs as the damp, draughty houses of our ancestors.

Homes for bugs

Modern homes provide ideal living conditions for many bugs. Many houses are centrally-heated, providing an even temperature throughout the year. Often, they are carpeted so there are comfortable places for the bugs to hide. And we produce lots of waste in various forms, ready to feed the bugs that share our homes. Tiny crumbs and food splashes can feed millions of bacteria.

Our warm, comfortable homes provide a welcoming habitat to bacteria and other microbes. Millions of them live in carpets, curtains and furniture.

Healthy Victorians

Our Victorian ancestors believed in lots of fresh air and unheated bedrooms. Spring cleaning was an important part of their life — they aired bedding and cleaned carpets thoroughly. Once the Victorians realised that disease was associated with the presence of dirt, they became obsessed with cleaning their homes, even though in those days there were no convenient vacuum cleaners or modern cleaning chemicals.

MICRO FACTS

Smelly flowers

You probably do not realise that bugs are all around you because you cannot see them. But you even get bugs in a vase of flowers. Once the flowers have stood in water for a few days, the water becomes cloudy and begins to smell. This is because it is full of bacteria.

Millions of bugs

In some ways, the Victorians were more successful than us because modern homes with double glazing do not allow bacteria and viruses carried in the air to escape, while central heating means that mites in the carpets and bedding are not killed off by the cold. Bugs can build up in huge numbers in the air, especially when someone has a cold. One sneeze can shoot out more than 10 million bacteria and even more viruses. Some people do not like the dry atmosphere caused by cental heating so they use a humidifier to put some moisture back into the air. The bugs love this! They can live in the humidifier or air conditioning system, which conveniently pumps bug-filled air all round the home.

Modern homes with central heating and double glazing allow microbes to thrive and prevent them from escaping outside.

Mites and wheezes

Did you know that your bedroom is infested with millions of tiny eight-legged relatives of spiders? And that the living room carpet and the sofa are also packed with them? Every home has them and normally they do us no harm.

Dust mites look like tiny fat spiders. They live in your carpet, and especially in pillows and bedding, where your skin flakes are a convenient food supply.

Human dust

House dust mites live in most houses and they love the warm conditions in bedrooms. This is handy for them because they feed on tiny pieces of skin that flake off your body surface. You shed 5—10 g of skin flakes every week. Mites live in the dust that builds up in mattresses, pillows, bedding and fabrics around the home. Eighty per cent of this dust is made up of skin flakes. House dust mites are tiny (0.2—0.3 mm) and you probably would not be able to see them without a microscope.

Dusty poo

By themselves, house dust mites are harmless; it is their waste that is the problem. A mite produces 20 pellets of faeces (poo) every day, which adds up to 200 times its own body weight during its whole life. Many people are allergic to these tiny pellets, which are spread through the air and breathed in as we toss and turn at night. People with house dust mite allergies suffer from wheezing, sneezing and itchy eyes. Some people are more seriously affected and develop asthma, which can make it hard to breathe. Most cases of asthma are thought to be caused by contact with house mite droppings. When people have allergies and asthma, great care must be taken to reduce the amount of dust by careful cleaning, putting protective covers on mattresses and having hard flooring instead of carpet in the bedroom.

▶

A sample of household dust, seen under a powerful microscope. It contains all sorts of debris, including mite faeces.

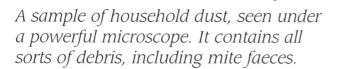

Nasty thoughts!

You probably share your bed with anything up to 10 million mites — ten per cent of the weight of a two-year-old mattress is made up of dead mites and their waste. Household carpet has been shown to be five times filthier than a busy street! It is packed with grit, dirt, bits of skin, various types of bugs and their faeces, and millions of bacteria.

Mite attack

Dust mites are not the only type of mite to find our homes a convenient place to live. Mites can attack our food, pets and plants.

Mites can infect both wild birds and pet birds, such as this cockatiel. They suck blood and weaken the bird, causing itching and the loss of feathers. ▼

🔷 Food attack

The mites that feed on stored food in the home are unpleasant, but they do not cause health problems except in a few people who are strongly allergic to them. The larger relative of the house dust mites may feed on ripe cheese, producing a greyish crust on the outside. Other similar mites feed on spilled flour or dried pasta, and yet others live on the outside of stored salami. If you have a pet bird, its cage may contain mites that feed on shed feathers and sometimes attack the bird itself. This makes the bird look very ruffled and uncomfortable, and causes it to shed even more feathers.

🔻 Red peril

You may not realise that there may be mites on your house plants. In hot, dry conditions, plants are attacked by red spider mites that suck the plant juices. These plant mites are bigger than other types of mite and you can sometimes find them hiding under yellowing leaves. Their bright red, spider-like body is about the size of a pinhead.

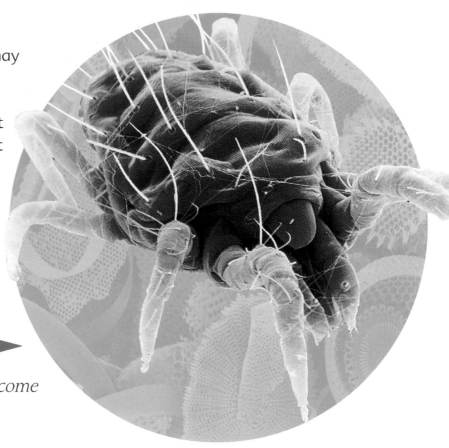

Red spider mites often attack house plants that are kept too dry. The plant's leaves often become yellow and may fall off.

MICRO FACTS

House plant attack

Apart from mites, many other tiny organisms attack house plants. You can sometimes see greenfly crawling over stems and leaves. They are easily removed with plant sprays, but scale insects are harder to detect. Look for tiny green cones like miniature limpets stuck tightly to the plant leaves and stems. These sap-suckers clamp themselves to the plant and feed on its juices, protected by their covering shell. They are hard to get rid of and may need to be picked off, one at a time.

Home hygiene

Most people spend a lot of time cleaning their kitchens, but however careful you are, you cannot get rid of all the bugs. However, you soon build up resistance to most of them.

Sink threat

Most kitchen bugs are concentrated around the sink, although they also cover the work surfaces and especially cutting boards where food is chopped up. Bacteria love living in the cloths or sponges used to scrub your plates and cups. The amount of bacteria they contain is incredible. Five millilitres (a teaspoonful) of water squeezed from a kitchen sponge has been found to contain up to 50 million bacteria. You cannot tell that they are there, although when a cloth is extremely contaminated it may smell bad.

Bug resistance

Some plastic products have disinfectants added to them to prevent bacteria growing on them. However, this may not be such a good thing, because after a long time bacteria may be able to resist the disinfectant and so cannot be killed off. It has been found that 86% of cases of food poisoning in the UK were caused by bugs in the home.

▲ *Food preparation surfaces and chopping boards can be home to millions of bacteria, and need very careful cleaning.*

Cleaning up

Bacteria live in huge numbers around the sink drain, feeding on tiny pieces of food waste. They are hard to dislodge because they form a sticky film over the surface. Some bacteria have a protective coat called a spore that protects them from drying out and from the effects of most cleaning agents and disinfectants. Powerful and dangerous chemicals such as bleach are the only way to get rid of all of them, but, even so, they soon return.

Warning: Bleach contains some powerful and dangerous chemicals. Never use bleach yourself. Only an adult should use it.

▲ *Hot tap water removes many bacteria, but the hotter water in a dishwasher can get rid of nearly all of them.*

MICRO FACTS

Rough, tough toothpaste

Did you know that the fossil shells of tiny creatures called diatoms are used in your home? Diatoms are minute organisms known as protista. Their tiny round shells contain a hard material called silica, and their remains are often included in liquid household cleaners, because the shells scour dirt from work surfaces. They are also used in some toothpaste to scrape the film of bacteria from your teeth.

Allergies

Do you sometimes find yourself sneezing or wheezing, even though you do not have a cold? If so, you might have an allergy.

A sunny summer's day can cause misery to hay fever sufferers because the pollen in the air causes them to sneeze and their eyes to water. ▼

What is an allergy?

Allergies occur when the body reacts to a perfectly harmless substance as if it were dangerous to health. The body attacks the allergy just as fiercely as it would fight an infection. Some of the substances the body produces in this counter-attack can cause irritation in the nose and eyes, or make you wheezy.

TRY IT YOURSELF

Allergy survey

How many of your school friends have an allergy? Ask them if they know of anything that makes them sneeze or wheeze, or have runny eyes. The causes might be house dust, pollen, pets or even strong sun or hot weather. See if these problems only happen at certain times of the year. If so, their sneezing might be caused by pollen or mould spores.

Pollen allergies

Some people are allergic to flowers and plants, even indoors. Pollen, released from trees, flowers and grasses in warm weather, floats in from outdoors. The microscopic pollen spores drift everywhere and are easily breathed in. As the body attacks them, the lining of the nose becomes sore and makes people sneeze. The substances produced by the body may also make the eyes water and itch. This common condition is called hay fever. Pollen breathed into the lungs can make the tiny air tubes tighten up, which makes some people feel wheezy.

▲ *Many activities produce large amounts of dust that can cause an allergic attack.*

Other causes of allergy

Tiny spores that are released from moulds and fungi growing on damp walls or decaying food cause allergies in some people. House dust mite faeces, which are about the same size as pollen grains, are a very common cause of allergy. It is quite common to sneeze when someone is dusting, or when bedding is shaken out, because this releases lots of the dusty mite faeces. Even pet animals can cause problems. Dust from dog and cat hair, or from the feathers of pet birds, are all common causes of allergy in the home.

▲ *Dust from pet animals commonly causes allergy, and may even be a cause of asthma.*

Down the toilet

We know that kitchens are home to huge numbers of bacteria and other microbes, so how safe do think your toilet is? Do you think toilets contain even more bacteria?

▲ *Toilets need careful cleaning because the microbes they contain can cause diseases such as food poisoning and diarrhoea.*

⬡ Dangerous flush

Actually, the toilet contains far fewer bacteria than the average kitchen sink, despite the huge number of microbes that we deposit there every time we use it. But every time you flush the toilet, an invisible cloud of bacteria and viruses is produced that floats around the bathroom for at least two hours. For this reason, the toilet must be cleaned regularly with disinfectant.

⬡ Clearing up

Watery and solid waste flushed down the toilet are carried along sewer pipes under the ground to a sewage treatment works. Here, the watery material is filtered off, and the solid remains are treated to make them safe. The watery material needs to be cleaned still further to make it safe, too. We rely on some helpful microbes to carry out this process.

Sewage waste is treated in huge ▶ *tanks where 'good' microbes are used to make it harmless.*

⬡ Hard-working bacteria

These specially-grown microbes, known as cultures, are added to the liquid, which is then stirred or sprayed in huge ponds so that oxygen in the air can get to it. The oxygen encourages the bugs to work quickly. After a time, with the help of chemical treatments, the waste is broken down completely to make it harmless. The bacteria that have worked to make the sewage safe form a sticky material called sludge, which sinks to the bottom while the clean water flows off the top.

When air is pumped into sewage, the 'good' microbes can work more effectively, breaking down the waste. ▼

MICRO FACTS

Good enough to drink

The liquid that is left after sewage has been purified is usually pumped back into rivers because, once the poisonous waste materials have been removed, it is safe enough for fish to live in it. Water treatment specialists say that it is safe enough to drink, too!

Clean drinking water

Clean drinking water is very important for health. It is a lack of clean water that causes disease in many less-developed countries.

Killing the bugs

If the bugs found in your faeces enter the water supply, they can cause disease. Water treatment plants pump chlorine into the drinking water to kill these bacteria (chlorine is the chemical you smell in swimming pools). The water is then carefully filtered through fine sand to remove any cloudiness and make it safe to drink.

◀

Water from the tap is treated with chlorine to make it safe. You can sometimes smell the chlorine slightly when you turn on the tap.

Making water safe

Some drinking water is pumped out of the ground from springs, while other water is taken from rivers. In London, most of the drinking water is pumped from the muddy River Thames, which shows the effectiveness of the filtering. In fact, every glass of water drunk by Londoners is continually being cleaned and re-used. In other places, water is collected in dams or pumped directly from the ground, but it always needs to be purified.

TRY IT YOURSELF

Can you taste the difference?

Can you tell the difference between tap water and bottled water? Which do you prefer? Pour an equal amount of tap water and one or more brands of bottled water into separate cups. Label them 1, 2, 3 and so on. Taste each one and see if you can detect any differences in flavour. Can you tell which water is which? Which one do you prefer?

Water and disease

Diseases such as typhoid and cholera once killed thousands of people because sewage contaminated the drinking water. These diseases are now very rare in developed countries, where the drinking water is almost bug-free. Sometimes, however, there are rare disease outbreaks caused by different types of bugs. One bug called Cryptosporidium has recently begun to cause disease because it is difficult to kill it off using chlorine and the usual methods of water treatment. In less-developed countries where water is not purified, typhoid, cholera and other diseases are still spread by untreated water that has been contaminated by sewage. Boiling the water can kill the bacteria causing these diseases.

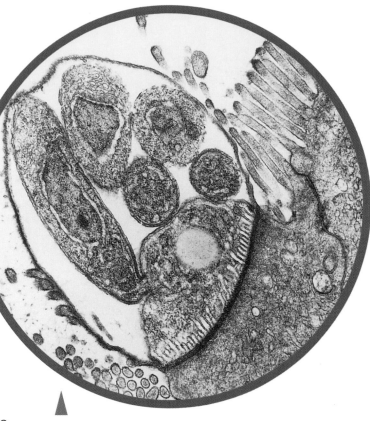

The Cryptosporidium parasite causes serious sickness and diarrhoea. It sometimes contaminates drinking water and is hard to remove. This picture shows the parasite attacking the gut wall.

Smelly water

Occasionally, water pumped from wells looks and smells odd. It may be a yellow or brown colour, or may smell like bad eggs. These problems are caused by harmless but unpleasant bacteria that release brownish iron into the water, staining it or producing sulphur, which smells bad. In some areas, the brownish colour is caused by perfectly harmless water that has filtered through peat before it reaches your tap.

This pump supplies much-needed water, but it may carry microbes that cause disease unless it is boiled.

Handy bugs

You may think that microbes are nasty or perhaps bad for your health, but they can be very useful. There are hundreds of materials around your home that contain or are made by microbes — usually bacteria.

Medicine

If you have had a serious infection caused by bacteria, you may have been treated with an antibiotic. Many antibiotics are natural substances that are produced by bacteria and moulds, and they kill other bacteria and fungi.

Antibiotics can be prepared from bugs grown in huge containers where their food is pumped in to make them grow quickly.

Insulin can be prepared from specially treated E. coli bacteria that normally live in the gut and sometimes cause disease. It is injected by many people with diabetes. ▶

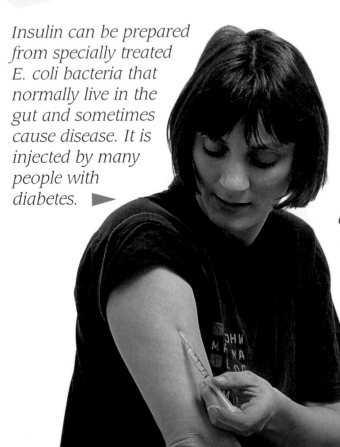

There are hundreds of these germ-killing substances known to science. Several types of bacteria or moulds are grown in huge vats, from which the antibiotics are collected. Another type of bacteria in our bodies can also help us to keep healthy. This bacteria produces a chemical called insulin, which controls sugar levels. People who are unable to produce insulin suffer from diabetes, and they need to inject themselves with a substitute. This insulin is made by special bacteria that have been changed or 'engineered'.

Additives

Many food additives are produced by bacteria, too, including sweeteners and flavour enhancers. Everyday foods such as yoghurt and cheese are produced by bacteria in a process called fermentation. A similar process is used to make beer and wine, using tiny fungi called yeast to break down sugar into alcohol. Yeast is also used to make dough rise in the preparation of traditional bread.

TRY IT YOURSELF

What does your food contain?

Look at the packages of food in your kitchen cupboards. Examine the list of ingredients and note how many contain artificial sweeteners or flavour enhancers. These may be made from safe bacteria.

▲ *These tiny grains of washing powder contain enzymes produced by bacteria that help break down stains and grease during washing.*

Dirt digesters

Enzymes are natural substances that help to digest other materials. Our bodies use enzymes in our digestive systems to break down the food we eat. Bacteria also produce enzymes to break down complicated food substances into simple chemicals that can be easily absorbed. Enzymes produced by bacteria have many different uses, such as removing stains from clothes, tenderising meat, cleaning moulds, bleaching stone-washed jeans and making strong detergents or biological washing powders. Sometimes, the powerful enzymes in biological washing powders can irritate people's skin.

21

Bug clean-up

Bacteria can attack just about anything, so we can put them to good use in clearing up the huge amounts of rubbish that we produce.

▲ *Rubbish is dumped in landfill sites where microbes break most of it down in a process than can take many years.*

MICRO FACTS

A long rot

How long does it take for common materials to rot into a harmless form?

2—5 months	6 months	1—12 years	10—20 years	50—100 years	Almost forever!
Paper	Orange peel	Cigarette ends	Plastic bags	Food cans	Glass and plastic bottles

⬡ Bugs in the dump

Much of our rubbish gets dumped into landfill sites — huge pits that have been left after gravel or other minerals have been dug out. Bacteria and fungi attack the rubbish, releasing enzymes that soften and digest the solid materials so they can be attacked by other organisms.

⬡ Rotting rubbish

Some materials, such as vegetable waste, rot down quickly. Other materials, like wood and paper (which is made from shredded wood), take longer, usually after fungi have begun the process of softening the tough wood fibres. The rubbish is slowly broken down to harmless forms, and at the same time large amounts of a gas called methane are released. Sometimes methane can be seen burning above a landfill site, producing a ghostly blue flame.

⬠ Recycling

Paper can be collected and treated so it can be used again. Glass can be collected and melted down for re-use, but recycling plastic is more difficult. To help solve this problem, scientists have now developed plastics that are biodegradable. This means that they can be broken down quickly by bugs such as bacteria and fungi. Modern plastic bottles and other useful objects can be made that look and work just like older plastic materials, but which will break down harmlessly once dumped into a landfill. Some of these plastics are made from substances that are extracted from other types of bacteria.

◄ *Rubbish is sorted by hand or machines to separate materials that can be recycled. What is left will be burned or dumped into landfills.*

TRY IT YOURSELF

Can it be recycled?

Many plastic products have symbols printed on them that say what kind of plastic they are. These symbols tell you whether the plastic can be recycled or not. Try to find a plastic product in your home that can be recycled.

Mouldy homes

Have you ever noticed black stains on the walls of a kitchen or bathroom? Or slimy dark patches on a shower curtain? These are mould, which is a form of fungus.

Mould spores

Moulds live on almost any damp surface. They grow from microscopic spores that drift through the air and come to rest in a damp place where there is something for them to feed on.

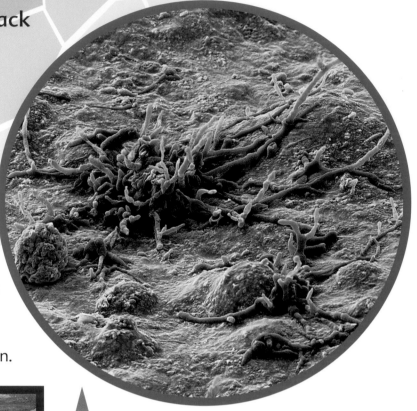

These tiny threads of fungi are growing on damp paper, where they produce discoloured patches.

Mould grows very quickly on bread when it becomes stale, producing colonies of green, grey or black fungus. It is made up of a mat of tangled threads called hyphae, which are too small to be seen without a microscope. Blackish mould grows on damp plaster, wallpaper or almost any other surface. It not only looks unpleasant, but it can also be a health risk for some people. The tiny spores can be breathed in, and substances on their surface may cause bad allergies in many people, making them sneeze and wheeze. Many people with asthma find that these spores can trigger an asthma attack.

Patches of dark mould often grow on damp walls, affecting wallpaper and plaster.

Paper damage

Mould also commonly attacks paper. You can see this in some very old books, as well as books that have been kept in a damp place. The mould produces stains that spread across the pages. You may also see the mould appearing in old pictures that are printed on paper. The paste that is used to fix modern wallpaper to the wall contains a fungicide, a special chemical that helps to stop fungus growing on the surface of the wallpaper.

Paste it up

The fungicide in wallpaper paste contains a chemical that prevents mould growing on damp walls. To see how it works, take several small pieces of paper and wet them under the tap. Leave one piece untreated, coat another piece with ordinary paste like the one you use at school, and another with a little wallpaper paste (wash your hands carefully after handling this). Put all three pieces of paper in a plastic bag and seal it with a rubber band. After a few days, mould will begin to grow. Which paper does the mould grow on? You can repeat this experiment with a flour and water paste, and with other types of glue. Always dispose of the bag without opening it.

Wet and dry rot

Fungi can get into your home in other ways, too. Spores find their way through cracks in paintwork, which also allow rainwater to get in and soak the wood. Fungi then grow through the wood, breaking it down and making it very weak. This is called wet rot and it is often seen in wooden window frames. But far worse is dry rot, where the fungus produces long strands that can completely destroy wood, making it crumble away. Usually, dry rot only affects very old houses, where it may work away for years before causing damage to large parts of the building.

◄

Dry rot can damage the structure of a house when fungi destroy staircases and wooden beams.

Hot water bugs

Washing with hot water gets rid of bugs. Or does it? There are some bacteria that grow in hot water, and they can make some people very ill.

The Legionella bacteria may live in hot water tanks, shower heads and air-conditioning systems. ▼

● Legionnaires' disease

The danger from these bugs was only discovered in 1976, when a group of American ex-servicemen were taken seriously ill at a meeting in the USA. They had a very severe form of pneumonia (a lung disease), and it proved very hard to treat. After a great deal of detective work, scientists traced the outbreak of disease to a type of bacteria that they called *Legionella*. These unusual bacteria live in water and are fairly common in soil and puddles. But they are different from other bacteria because they love hot water, where they grow rapidly. The *Legionella* bacteria were found in the air-conditioning plant at the hotel where the disease struck, and were pumped out into the hotel rooms in water droplets that were inhaled by the guests.

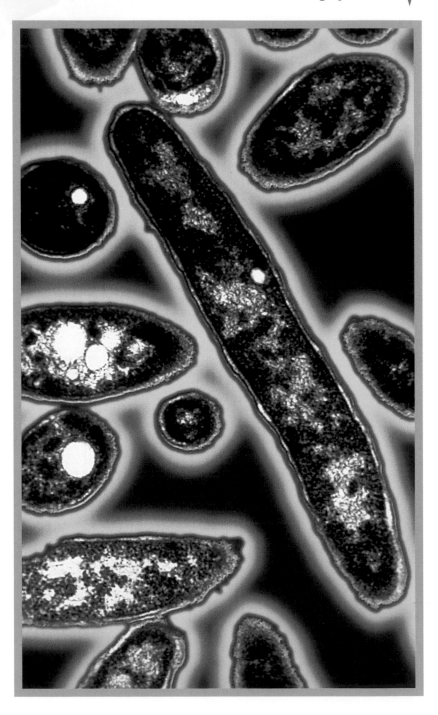

⬢ Dangerous — but rare

Since then there have been a few other outbreaks, usually blamed on faulty air-conditioning systems. But the bacteria can live anywhere that hot water accumulates, such as shower heads and jacuzzis, if these are not properly looked after and cleaned. Although the bugs are quite common, the conditions in which they grow in large numbers in hot stagnant water and are sprayed out in tiny water droplets do not occur often, so the disease is quite rare.

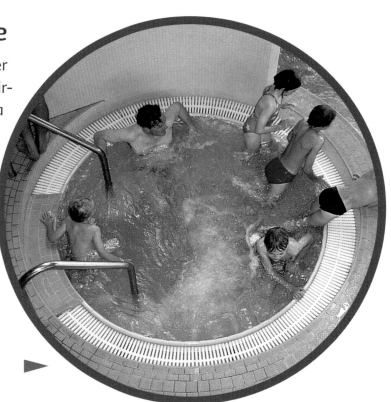

The Legionella bug can thrive in the hot water of jacuzzis and hot tubs if they are not carefully cleaned.

MICRO FACTS

Disease attack

An outbreak of Legionnaires' disease in Barrow-in-Furness, in England, in 2002, affected more than 100 people. They were infected outdoors as they moved along a walkway leading to a carpark. Unfortunately, an infected cooling system blew air containing the microbes directly at these people. As a result, they were forced to inhale the contaminated water droplets.

Air-conditioning plants make a suitable home for Legionella. The bugs can be pumped out in the moist air from the plants.

⬢ Who is affected?

Legionnaires' disease usually affects people who do not have a very good resistance to disease, such as old people or those who are already ill. It is also more common in people whose lungs have been affected by smoking. You cannot catch the disease from another person, but only by breathing in the contaminated water droplets. It can be treated with powerful antibiotics.

Bigger bugs

Lots of bigger creatures share your home, although you will seldom see them. Usually, they do not cause any serious risk to health, but they are a nuisance and most people do not like them around.

The woodworm beetle is 4-6 mm long and is rarely seen. Its larvae often bore into the wood and leave small holes when they emerge as adults, having tunnelled through the wood and caused a lot of damage.

Woodworm

You might see lots of tiny holes in a piece of old wooden furniture. These have been made by woodworms. They are the grubs (larvae) of tiny beetles that feed on wood, and they can gnaw away most of the wood without anyone realising that they are there. It is only when they emerge as little beetles that they make the tiny hole that tells you that woodworms are present.

MICRO FACTS
What is a bookworm?

If your nose is always buried in a book, people may call you a 'bookworm'. But did you know that there really are such creatures, although they are properly called book lice? These are tiny flattened insects, about 2 mm long, that live in books, chewing away at the paper and the binding. Book lice and other pests are most common in damp places, and can cause a lot of damage to old books. They seldom live in dry, modern homes.

Moth larvae

Small brown moths called clothes moths lay their eggs on woollen items, such as clothes. The eggs hatch into tiny grubs that eat the wool and leave holes in the clothes. Some people use 'moth balls', which have a strong smell that keeps the moths away. Similar moth grubs sometimes live in woollen carpets, chewing away at the fibres.

Silverfish

Silverfish live in damp places such as bathrooms and under sinks. They are very shy and you will only see them if you disturb their hiding place, causing them to scuttle away very quickly. Silverfish are about 1 cm long and have a shiny grey colour. When disturbed, they run very fast with a wriggling movement like a fish. Silverfish are a nuisance because they nibble food, paper and fabric.

Often the first sign of fleas is when a pet is seen scratching constantly.
◀

Fleas

Fleas are more of a problem because they bite humans, causing itchy bumps, usually round your ankles. You will only get fleas in the home if you have a cat or dog because human fleas are increasingly rare in developed countries. Cat and dog fleas are quite happy to bite us, too, although they prefer their original home on your pets. The vet can supply flea treatments for pets, but this will not get rid of them from the home, because flea eggs drop on to the carpet, where they hatch into tiny grubs. They can live here for a long time before becoming adults.

The cat flea is a yellow creature that only lives on its host when feeding. At other times it is found in carpets. ▶

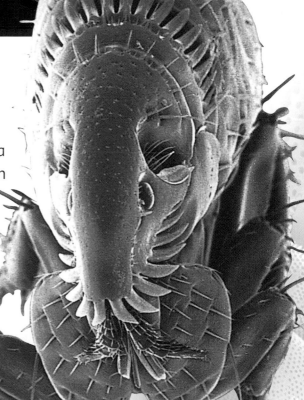

Glossary

Allergy: Condition in which the body reacts strongly against harmless substances such as pollen or house mite dust.

Antibiotic: Substance that kills or damages bacteria. Many antibiotics are produced by organisms; others can be made artificially in the laboratory.

Asthma: Condition where the breathing passages in the lungs become narrowed. It may resemble an extreme form of allergy, triggered by certain types of dust.

Bacteria: Tiny single-celled microbes that live nearly everywhere, including people's bodies, food and homes. Some bacteria can be 'good', for example, helping people to digest food. Other bacteria can be 'bad', because they cause diseases.

Biodegradable: Substance that can be broken down into a harmless form by micro-organisms.

Chlorine: Strong-smelling gas that is released from household bleach. Chlorine can kill almost all types of microbe.

Cholera: Very dangerous but rare disease of the gut that is caused by drinking water contaminated with sewage.

Decay: Process of breaking down dead material by microbes.

Diabetes: Disease caused when the pancreas stops making the hormone insulin, affecting the way in which the body handles sugar in our food.

Diatom: Single-celled organism, with a shell made of a glassy material called silica. It is a very common fossil.

Disinfectant: Liquid used to kill harmful micro-organisms.

Enzyme: Natural substance that helps the digestion of food materials.

Faeces: Solid waste that animals excrete after digesting food.

Fermentation: Process in which microbes break down a food substance, changing its appearance or taste.

Flagella: Thin hair-like strands found on some bacteria and other microbes. They may allow the microbe to move about.

Flea: Tiny jumping insect, usually found on cats, that also bites people to feed on their blood.

Fungus: Organism that breaks down dead material and sometimes also causes diseases. Most fungi are microscopic; others are large, like mushrooms.

Hay fever: Condition in which the body reacts strongly against pollen that is breathed in, causing inflammation of the nose, sneezing and runny eyes.

House dust mites: Tiny spider-like organisms that feed on human skin flakes. Their droppings can cause asthma.

Humidifier: Machine that pumps out damp air.

Hygiene: Measures to preserve our health by controlling the level of microbes around us. These include washing our hands and cleaning kitchen work surfaces.

Hyphae: Tiny threads of fungus that penetrate the soil or food materials.

Immunity: Condition in which the body can fight off microbes after once being infected.

Infection: Condition in which a microbe grows inside another organism. An infection can be harmless so it is not necessarily a disease.

Insulin: Substance produced in the body that controls how we use sugar in our food. In the disease diabetes, insulin is no longer produced and may need to be injected regularly.

Landfill site: Pit or disused quarry that is used to dispose of large amounts of rubbish. Once filled, the landfill site is covered with earth, and trees and grass are planted to restore the appearance of the land.

Larvae: Immature form of insects or other animals.

Legionnaires' disease: Infection caused by bacteria that can grow in hot water systems.

Methane: Colourless, odourless gas that is often produced during the process of decay. It sometimes catches fire and burns with a blue flame.

Microbe (micro-organism): Microscopic organism.

Mites: Tiny spider-like animals that feed on skin flakes, food debris, or sometimes on ourselves.

Mould: Tiny thread-like fungi that cause food decay.

Oxygen: Colourless gas in the air we breathe.

Pollen: Male spores produced by a flowering plant.

Recycling: Re-use of household and other wastes.

Sewage: Waste material that is drained from the toilet.

Silica: Glassy substance that makes up the shell of diatoms. Sand is made mostly of silica.

Spore: Cell surrounded by a tough shell that stops it from drying out. Bacteria, fungi and ferns all reproduce by means of spores.

Typhoid: Serious bacterial infection of the gut that can be picked up from food contaminated with human wastes.

Virus: Very simple organism that can only grow and reproduce inside a living cell. All viruses are parasites.

Further information

The following websites contain lots of useful information about microbes and the way they can affect the home:

Microbes — invisible invaders, amazing allies:
www.miamisci.org/microbes/facts18.html

Microbe Zoo:
http://commtechlab.msu.edu/sites/dlc-me/zoo

Microbiology on-line:
www.microbiologyonline.org.uk/wom.htm

Stalking the mysterious microbe:
www.microbe.org

Bacteria and technology:
www.earthlife.net/prokaryotes/technology.html

Microbe World:
www.microbeworld.org

Microbes in sickness and in health:
www.niaid.nih.gov/publications/microbes.htm

Biological pollutants in the home:
www.cpsc.gov/CPSCPUB/PUBS/425.html

Sponges and sinks and rags:
www.sciencenews.org/sn_arch/9_14_96/bob2.htm

The house dust mite:
www-micro.msb.le.ac.uk/video/mite.html

Legionnaires' disease: a history:
http://news.bbc.co.uk/1/hi/health/2169042.stm

Creepy things:
www.knaw.nl/ecpa/expo/insects.htm

Sewage treatment:
www.dcs.ex.ac.uk/water/sewage.htm

Antibacterials and disinfectants: are they necessary?:
www.checnet.org/healthehouse/education/articles-detail.asp?Main_ID=121

index

First published in 2003
by Franklin Watts
96 Leonard Street
LONDON EC2A 4XD

Franklin Watts Australia
45–51 Huntley Street
Alexandria
NSW 2015

© 2003 Franklin Watts

A CIP catalogue record for this book is available from the British Library.

ISBN: 0 7496 4791 4
Printed in Hong Kong, China

Editor: Kate Banham
Designer: Joelle Wheelwright
Art direction: Peter Scoulding
Illustration: Ian Thompson
Picture research: Diana Morris
Educational consultant: Dot Jackson

Acknowledgements

The publishers would like to thank the following for permission to reproduce photographs in this book: Adina Tovy Amsel/Eye Ubiquitous: 12. Alex Bartel/SPL: 27b. Bob Battersby/Eye Ubiquitous: 6. Dr. Jeremy Burgess/SPL: 11t, 11b. Dorothy Burrows/Eye Ubiquitous: 27t. Phillip Carr/Photofusion: 23br. Janice Carstairs/Eye Ubiquitous: 22. CDC/SPL: 2t, 26. CNRI/SPL: 3c. Eye of Science/SPL: 3b, 24t. John Howard/SPL: 25b. Paul Hutley/Eye Ubiquitous: 15b. Sally Lancaster/Photofusion: 4c, 16. Frank Lane Picture Agency: 29t. London School of Hygiene & Tropical Medicine/SPL: 19t. C. Macpherson/Photofusion: 18. Selby McCreery/Eye Ubiquitous: 4b, 5b. Cordelia Molloy/SPL: 14. Yiorgos Nikiteas/Eye Ubiquitous: 13t. Sue Passmore/Eye Ubiquitous: 15t. Chris Priest & Mark Clark/SPL: 20b. Geoff Redmayne/Eye Ubiquitous: 7t. Rosenfeld Images/SPL: 17b. Colin Seddon/RSPCA Photo Library: 10. SPL: front cover br, 3t, 13b, 29b. Paul Seheult/Eye Ubiquitous: 23bl, 24b. Andrew Syred/SPL: front cover tl & bl, b cover tl & cr, 2b, 8, 9t, 21, 28t. Julia Waterlow/Eye Ubiquitous: 19b. Elizabeth Whiting: 7b. Kevin Wilton/Eye Ubiquitous: 17t. Ed Young/SPL: 20t.

Whilst every attempt has been made to clear copyright, should there be any inadvertent omission please apply in the first instance to the publisher regarding rectification.